A Quick Guide to…

Using Gender-Sensitive Indicators

Tony Beck

Commonwealth Secretariat

Gender Management System Series

Gender Management System Handbook

Using Gender-Sensitive Indicators: A Reference Manual for Governments and Other Stakeholders

Gender Mainstreaming in Development Planning: A Reference Manual for Governments and Other Stakeholders

Gender Mainstreaming in Finance: A Reference Manual for Governments and Other Stakeholders

Gender Mainstreaming in the Public Service: A Reference Manual for Governments and Other Stakeholders

Gender Mainstreaming in Education: A Reference Manual for Governments and Other Stakeholders

Gender Mainstreaming in Trade and Industry: A Reference Manual for Governments and Other Stakeholders

Gender Mainstreaming in Agriculture and Rural Development: A Reference Manual for Governments and Other Stakeholders

Gender Mainstreaming in Information and Communications: A Reference Manual for Governments and Other Stakeholders

Gender and Equal Employment Opportunities: A Reference Manual for Governments and Other Stakeholders

A Quick Guide to the Gender Management System

A Quick Guide to Using Gender-Sensitive Indicators

A Quick Guide to Gender Mainstreaming in Development Planning

A Quick Guide to Gender Mainstreaming in Finance

A Quick Guide to Gender Mainstreaming in the Public Service

A Quick Guide to Gender Mainstreaming in Education

A Quick Guide to Gender Mainstreaming in Trade and Industry

A Quick Guide to Gender Mainstreaming in Agriculture and Rural Development

A Quick Guide to Gender Mainstreaming in Information and Communications

A Quick Guide to Gender and Equal Employment Opportunities

Commonwealth Secretariat
Marlborough House
Pall Mall, London SW1Y 5HX,
United Kingdom

© Commonwealth Secretariat,
June 1999

Designed and published by the Commonwealth Secretariat.
Printed in the United Kingdom by Abacus Direct.
Wherever possible, the Commonwealth Secretariat uses paper sourced from sustainable forests or from sources that minimise a destructive impact on the environment.

Copies of this publication can be ordered direct from:

Vale Packaging Ltd,
420 Vale Road, Tonbridge, Kent
TN9 1TD, United Kingdom
Tel: + 44 (0)1732 359387
Fax: +44 (0) 1732 770620
e-mail: vale@vale-ltd.co.uk

Price: £5.99
0-85092-595-9

Web sites:
http://www.thecommonwealth.org/gender
http://www.thecommonwealth.org
http://www.youngcommonwealth.org

Contents

List of Figures

List of Tables

Preface

In 1996, Commonwealth Ministers Responsible for Women's Affairs mandated the Commonwealth Secretariat to develop the concept of the Gender Management System (GMS), a comprehensive network of structures, mechanisms and processes for bringing a gender perspective to bear in the mainstream of all government policies, programmes and projects. The establishment and strengthening of gender management systems and of national women's machineries was the first of 15 government action points identified in the 1995 Commonwealth Plan of Action on Gender and Development.

This guide is intended to serve as an accessible reference manual to aid readers in using a GMS to mainstream gender in the public service ministry of national governments. It is an abridged version of the GMS publication *Using Gender-Sensitive Indicators: A Reference Manual for Governments and Other Stakeholders*, presenting the main points of that document in an accessible way. It is hoped that both documents will be used by policy-makers, planners, personnel managers, field staff and others.

These publications are part of the Gender Management System Series, which provides tools and sector-specific guidelines for gender mainstreaming. This guide is intended to be used in combination with other documents in the GMS Series, particularly the *Gender Management System Handbook*, which presents the conceptual and methodological framework of the GMS.

The development of the GMS Reference Manuals and Quick Guides has been a collaborative effort between the Commonwealth Secretariat's Gender and Youth Affairs Division and many individuals and groups. Their contributions to the thinking behind the GMS are gratefully acknowledged. In particular, I would like to thank the following: all those member governments who supported the development of the GMS and encouraged us to move the project forward; participants at the first GMS meeting in Britain in February 1997 and at the GMS Workshop in Malta in April 1998, who provided invaluable conceptual input and feedback; and the Steering Committee on the Plan of Action (SCOPA). I am also most grateful to: the consultants who worked on the guide, including Tony Beck, University of British Columbia, Canada, who wrote the text, and Daniel Woolford, Consultant Editor of the GMS Series, who revised and edited it for publication; and the staff of the Gender Affairs Department, Gender and Youth Affairs Division, Commonwealth Secretariat, particularly Ms Eleni Stamiris, former Director of the Division, who took the lead in formulating the GMS concept and mobilising the various stakeholders in its development, Dr Judith May-Parker who provided substantive editorial input, and Dr Rawwida Baksh-Soodeen, Project Co-ordinator of the GMS Series, who guided the project through to publication.

We hope that this resource series will be of genuine use to you in your efforts to mainstream gender.

Nancy Spence
Director
Gender and Youth Affairs Division
Commonwealth Secretariat

1 | Introduction and Overview

What are Gender-Sensitive Indicators and Why Are They Useful?

In efforts to advance equality and equity between women and men, there is a need to generate accurate and relevant data on the status of women, men and gender relations. This data helps make gender biases more visible and facilitates effective policy-making to bring about greater gender equality and equity.

The need for sex-disaggregated data has been stressed in numerous international conventions and declarations, including the 1995 Platform for Action of the Fourth UN World Conference on Women in Beijing and the 1995 Commonwealth Plan of Action on Gender and Development.

Statistics and indicators

An indicator is an item of data that summarises a large amount of information in a single figure, in such a way as to give an indication of change over time, and in comparison to a norm. Indicators differ from statistics in that, rather than merely presenting facts, indicators involve comparison to a norm in their interpretation.

A *gender-sensitive indicator* can be defined as an indicator that captures gender-related changes in society over time. Thus, whereas a gender statistic provides factual information about the status of women, a gender-sensitive indicator provides "direct evidence of the status of women, relative to some agreed normative standard or explicit reference group" (Johnson, 1985).

National-level gender-sensitive indicators are among the key means by which planners and policy-makers measure gender inequality. They also provide information on the basis of which gender specialists advocate for policies likely to lead to greater gender equality. Gender-sensitive indicators support the gender and development approach which focuses on changing the gendered nature of society through the promotion of gender equity, rather than on women in isolation, which was the focus of the women in development model and emphasises gender statistics.

Aim and Scope of this Guide

This guide is designed to assist the user in the selection, use and dissemination of gender-sensitive indicators at the national level. It should be of particular use to governments that are establishing and using a Gender Management System and/or developing a national data base on gender-sensitive indicators as well as NGOs, women's groups, professional associations, the academic community and others interested in promoting gender equality and equity.

Interpreting Indicators

Indicators, like any other methodological tool, have their limitations. Recognising these limitations is necessary for understanding what can and cannot be achieved by using them.

The major limitation of gender-sensitive indicators is that they do not provide information on wider social patterns: they usually say little about why gender relations have been shaped in a particular way and how these relations can be changed. They point to key questions rather than provide answers. Indicator systems should therefore be complemented by gender analysis, which involves examining, often at a micro-level, the social relations between women and men, and the structural features of society which reinforce gender inequality and inequity.

Another limitation concerns the accuracy of data. Most indicator systems are developed from national censuses. However, much of the data in national censuses is subject to various problems, including infrequent collection, sex bias, poor enumeration, and imprecise definition of key terms. In addition, because of differences in definitions of terminology between nations, indicators are often not comparable internationally. Census data should therefore be considered a pointer towards a certain trend rather than definitive evidence of that trend.

A key element in the use of indicators is to interpret correctly the normative element that is inherent in their construction. The same indicator may be interpreted differently in different settings. Care must therefore be taken in defining the norm or benchmark implicit in any indicator and against which change is measured. For example, in examining the status of women, is the norm the situation of men in a particular country, or is it women in other countries? Care must also be taken to ensure that when using indicators to compare gender equity across countries, the indicators have been collected using similar definitions of, for example, economic activity or literacy.

A further problem can be a lack of participation and cross-cultural dimensions. Recommendations for indicator systems and data sets are often developed by specialists, with limited participation from governments, NGOs or the general population. Indicators may therefore reflect the interests of a few experts rather than a general consensus; for this reason, as widespread participation in the development of indicators as is feasible should be encouraged.

Given these problems, caution should be exercised when using and interpreting indicators, especially when drawing cross-country conclusions.

2 Developing a National-Level Database of Gender-Sensitive Indicators

This section discusses the main sources for a national-level database on the status of women and gender equality, and suggests ways of increasing the gender sensitivity of these sources. It also provides information on training and methodological advice on gathering appropriate indicators.

Data Sources

There are three main data systems that produce indicators, which, if collected and interpreted correctly, can support national-level planning towards gender equality and equity. These are census surveys, the UN System of National Accounts (SNA), and sample surveys of the population.

At present, census surveys and sample surveys of the population collect sex-disaggregated data, although often not in a consistent fashion. Changes to guidelines for the SNA have increased its potential as a source for gender-sensitive indicators. No single source can provide all of the data needed by different countries and different users. Censuses, household surveys and registration and administrative data systems should be used to complement each other wherever possible. Although serious efforts have been made to enhance the gender-sensitivity of these data systems, in some cases improvements to current practices may be necessary to ensure that they are fully engendered.

Censuses and labour force surveys[1]

Censuses are the mainstay of the data gathering system and as such offer considerable opportunities for gathering gender-sensitive data. However, a UN review of the census and labour force survey practices of a number of developing countries in the period 1970 to 1990, in terms of concepts and definitions selected, uncovered certain problems (UN, 1993):

✦ In a number of censuses, interviewers are not sufficiently trained to identify women who are primarily housewives but who nevertheless work in activities related to the production of goods and services. The principle that participation in any economic activity should be counted, irrespective of any other activity, is often not applied.

✦ The concept of 'usually active population' is unclear and not effectively articulated in national censuses. This concept is important for the inclusion of women's work which may be seasonal and only captured through use of a longer reference period.

✦ The ways in which questions about work are asked can significantly affect census results. Words such as 'employment', 'job', 'work' or 'main activity' can mean different things to different people. For example, a national sample survey in Kenya in 1974 revealed that activity rates for married women ages 20 to 49 varied from about 20 per cent to about 90 per cent depending on whether the key word in the questionnaire was 'job' or 'work'. A 'job' was regarded as a paid wage or salary employment, whereas 'work' was more broadly interpreted to include virtually all time-consuming activities required for the family's survival.

Over the last ten years extensive work has been done on making censuses and labour surveys more gender-sensitive, particularly in the area of women's paid and unpaid work, which is a key area where governments can improve their performance. Questions in censuses and labour force surveys should be carefully framed so that women's contributions are included wherever possible. Questions regarding economic activity should follow UN and ILO recommendations. Questions related to women's work should include both paid and unpaid work. Extensive education for enumerators and the general population as to the meaning of the term 'work' may be necessary before women's contributions can be fully captured.

These are some recommendations for improving census surveys so as to reduce gender bias[2]:

✦ Experience has illustrated the need for training and gender sensitisation of interviewers. Interviewers should receive consistent training, i.e., all trainers should transmit the same instructions to their trainees. Particular attention should be paid to the training of interviewers in asking the questions, since the possibility of introducing response and non-response biases is very strong when concepts are difficult to understand and/or interpret. For example, male interviewers may have difficulty with the concept that many of the activities carried out by women constitute work.

+ Surveys need to be carried out in a participatory fashion or at least have a participatory element.

+ The use is recommended of a building block approach, whereby a series of questions are asked so as to exclude those persons who do not qualify for inclusion in the particular topic, leaving those who, by definition, are entitled to be included.

+ Language in the census should be non-sexist. For example, questions in the census should focus on additional questions to 'main activity' in societies where women's place is considered to be in the home.

+ Instruction manuals should be developed so as to adequately inform the interviewer which concepts should be applied.

+ The seasonal patterns of women's work should be taken into account.

+ Male interviewers may have particular problems interviewing women. In order to establish the nature of women's participation, more women interviewers should be employed.

+ Typical general key word questions, as used in censuses and labour force surveys around the world, were found to be inadequate. More detailed key work questions or preferably activity schedules should be used, and where this is not feasible in censuses (because of limitations on numbers of words), separate labour force surveys should be carried out.

+ The collection of information on multiple labour force activities should be encouraged. Unless such data are collected, it is likely that the true extent of female labour force activity in rural areas of developing countries will continue to be grossly under-reported.

+ Additional methodological work on the collection of time use data should be encouraged.

In producing and using gender-sensitive indicators for policy purposes, two other priority areas are women's work in agriculture and women's work in the informal sector. In both areas there is serious under-reporting in official statistics of women's contributions.[3]

Household surveys

Due to the limits to the number of questions in censuses, their focus on a few topics, the ten-year time gap between many censuses and their formal mode, censuses and other national-level surveys usually provide very little information about household dynamics or gender relations. Censuses and other national level surveys must therefore be complemented by micro-level household surveys if a comprehensive picture relating to gender equality is to be built up.

Household surveys are surveys of a sample of the population (usually more than 2,000 households) focusing on a particular subject or subjects and with the household as the focus of investigation. They can be carried out at frequent intervals, say, quarterly. The size of these surveys makes them useful instruments for the generation of gender-sensitive indicators. In developing national level data sets, household surveys should focus specifically on areas where there are serious gaps in data. In particular, they should examine gender roles, household dynamics and decision-making, control of and access to economic and other resources, and violence against women.

The following guidelines should to be followed to ensure the successful implementation of a gender-sensitive household survey (UN, 1988a):

✦ There should be an existing household survey capability of some sort and hence a team with some practical experience of both field work and subsequent analysis.
✦ One or more persons with professional capacity and a personal interest in innovations to improve data on women should be involved.
✦ The possibility should be explored of carrying out small-scale pre-trial interviews to adapt suggestions to local conditions.
✦ A final sample of at least 2,000 households (or possibly 1,500 in a very homogeneous society) is recommended.
✦ The planning committee should have a significant representation of women members representing different ethnic, class/caste and age groups, and strong participation by persons who can be expected to use the data.
✦ There should be a possibility of providing training to the interviewers and of developing a core of female interviewers.

Time-use studies

Time-use studies can be included as part of a larger household survey or carried out separately. They are becoming increasingly useful in providing gender-sensitive indicators relating to women's and men's contributions. Two main, interrelated sets of concerns are usually investigated in these studies (UN, 1990b). The first covers the utilisation of human resources in the household and the second, the measurement of employment, unemployment and underemployment. There are four main types of time-use survey, all of which have strengths and limitations (UN, 1988a):

+ observation;
+ random instant measurement (a schedule of random visits which record what household members were doing just before the arrival of the investigator);
+ diaries; and
+ recall (usually based on a recall period of 24 hours).

Extensive research was undertaken for the 1995 *Human Development Report* on the amount of time women and men spend on market and non-market activities. This and other research points to the disproportionate load women bear in most societies.

As with any other approach, time-use studies are limited methodologically:

+ "Surveys that examine only the allocation of time by women and men during *workdays* tend to underestimate the contribution of women to economic activity because their work continues unabated during 'days off'. The same is true with surveys of economic activities *during the day*, since a significant portion of women's work occurs at night" (UNDP, 1995: 91).
+ "In developing countries, people do not think of their activities in terms of clock time, nor can they be expected to keep diaries listing their daily activities … Intensive observation and interview methods require well-trained and well-supervised interviewers and a great amount of interview time" (UN, 1990b: 57).
+ There may be lack of participation in survey design by those being studied.

Despite these problems, time-use studies are valuable in highlighting women's work and generating gender-sensitive indicators that can be used as part of a national data base. They can also be useful in the generation of satellite accounts on unpaid work.

System of National Accounts and unpaid work

The UN System of National Accounts (SNA) is used to measure production and growth in most countries, and since 1945 the SNA has been one of the central tools used for policy-making related to the working of a country's economic system. Implementing changes to the SNA is a key area where governments can improve the way in which gender-disaggregated data is collected and used.

Measures such as the SNA and GDP, with their concentration on measuring paid employment, have been strongly criticised for having a gender bias, and in particular for ignoring women's overall contribution to the economy and to society as a whole. Governments are advised to experiment with the formation of satellite accounts to the SNA, focusing initially on national time-use studies that measure the extent of unpaid work in the country. Methodologies for these studies should ideally be harmonised with international norms, where they exist.

CEDAW

States parties to the Convention on the Elimination of All Forms of Discrimination against Women (CEDAW) are required to submit reports every four years on all articles of CEDAW. Reporting on CEDAW offers governments an excellent opportunity to synthesise available gender-related data, to measure advancements in the status of women, and to identify and fill data gaps. While census and other national level surveys deal mainly with demography, work, health, and education, CEDAW provides an opportunity to produce gender-sensitive indicators on empowerment, violence against women, cultural issues and women's rights.

Methodological Advice

The following is a checklist of methodological points to bear in mind when using gender-sensitive indicators at the national level. An indicator or indicator system need not conform to all of the following, but the closer the conformity the more likely it is that it will be useful.

✦ **Comparison to a norm:** Use of gender-sensitive indicators should involve comparison to a norm, for example the situation of men in the same country or the situation of women in another country. In this way the indicator can focus on questions of gender equality and equity rather than only on the status of women.

✦ **Disaggregation:** Data should be disaggregated by sex. Wherever possible, national level indicators should also:
  – be disaggregated by age;
  – be disaggregated by socioeconomic grouping;
  – be disaggregated by national and/or regional origin;
  – note the time period;
  – note geographical coverage; and
  – note data sources.
  This kind of information can inform a broader analysis of the social forces that have brought about the specific status of women and men in a particular society.

✦ **Ease of access:** Data should be easy to use and understand. Indicators should be phrased in easily understandable language, and should be developed at a level relevant to the institutional capabilities of the country concerned.

✦ **Scope of availability:** Indicators should be available for the whole country.

✦ **Reliability:** Data should be relatively reliable. No data is absolutely reliable but reliability checks should be carried out. For example, findings from censuses should be compared to findings from micro-level studies for accuracy.

✦ **Measurability:** Indicators must be about something measurable. Concepts such as 'women's empowerment' or 'gender equity' may be difficult to define and measure. In this case proxy indicators, for example relating to greater choice for women in accessing health care or education, may be used instead of the less precise concepts.

✦ **Time-frames:** Gender-sensitive indicators should be reliable enough to use as a time series. The time span which the indicator covers should be clearly specified.

✦ **International comparability:** Gender-sensitive indicators should be collected using internationally accepted definitions. While these definitions are sometimes imprecise, they are usually the best terms available and allow for international comparison.

✦ **Measuring impact:** The indicator should, where possible, measure the outcome or impact of a situation rather than the input. For example, women's literacy is often a better measure of women's educational status than female enrolment rates because literacy measures the impact of enrolment rates. Similarly, female mortality rates are a better measure of women's health status than access to health facilities.

✦ **Participation:** Indicators should be used and developed in as participatory a process as possible. This will involve setting up inter-departmental government committees but also holding focus group meetings with the public and eliciting public opinion from women and men wherever possible.

Training for the Production of Gender-Sensitive Databases

Training related to gender-sensitive indicators is needed in two areas:
✦ training of statisticians, economists and others within the national level census and survey systems; and
✦ training of enumerators and researchers carrying out surveys at the local level.

In the first area, Ghana provides a useful example of advances that can be made:

"The Statistical Service recognises that the ability to produce reliable, timely and gender-sensitive statistics depends ... on the availability of highly trained and experienced personnel ... a comprehensive staff training programme, involving regular in-service training, training in local institutions of higher education and external training, has been introduced for both graduate and non-graduate staff to upgrade their skills."

Boateng, 1994: 103

In the second area, training of interviewers, Anker (1994: 71) provides two examples where training of enumerators led to a significant increase in coverage of women's labour force activity in large-scale surveys. In Argentina and Paraguay, labour force information was collected for over 1,000 women and men using two different interviewer training sessions, and where interviewer training (four sessions over two days) was found to have an important effect on the reporting of female labour force activity. In Egypt, training organised by the Egyptian statistical office provided significantly improved information on women's labour force activity.

Popular Participation in Indicator Collection and Use

Most work on gender-sensitive indicators continues to be non-participatory, in the sense that women in developing countries, particularly poor and marginalised women, are not included in the process whereby knowledge is generated and translated into policy. Given the importance of finding out more about the status of women and gender equity, a key goal for governments should be to facilitate popular participation in the generation of gender-related information.

One means of achieving this is through the use of qualitative indicators. These are essentially people's perceptions and views on a given subject. Two ways of distinguishing between quantitative and qualitative indicators are by the source of information and by the way in which this information is interpreted and used. Quantitative indicators focus on areas that are easy to quantify, such as wage rates or education levels, usually drawn from censuses or administrative records. Because of their focus on formal surveys they are usually interpreted using statistical methods. Qualitative indicators are usually obtained from participant observation, attitude surveys or anthropological field work, i.e., less formal surveys, and are often analysed in a descriptive fashion (CIDA, 1996b).

If used correctly, qualitative indicators can be an important means of facilitating popular participation in indicator use, because many surveys involving qualitative indicators are participatory in nature. Qualitative and quantitative indicators should complement each other and ensure the inclusion of different perspectives on a topic. In addition, a focus on qualitative indicators can help ensure that poor and marginalised women's views, which are often missed in formal surveys, can be taken into account. However, one danger to be avoided is equating qualitative indicators with women; if this occurs there may be a tendency to continue to consider such indicators as part of the female terrain and therefore as subjective, given past cultural constructs of women as 'subjective' and men as 'objective'.

Notes

1   This section draws on CIDA (1996a, 1996b); World Bank (1994); Westerndorff and Ghai (1993); and various UN documents.
2   See Anker *et al* (1988); UN (1993: 33-38); and the 1991 Indian census.
3   Further information on these two key areas can be found in UN (1995), UN (1993), UN (1990b) and Dixon-Mueller (1985). See also the Gender Management System publication *Gender Mainstreaming in Agriculture and Rural Development: A Reference Manual for Governments and Other Stakeholders*.

3 Gathering and Using Gender-Sensitive Indicators

This section examines a number of key areas for gender-sensitive indicators at the national level:
1 Population composition and change
2 Human settlements and geographical distribution
3 Households and families, marital status, fertility
4 Learning in formal and non-formal education
5 Health, health services, nutrition
6 Economic activity and labour force participation
7 Access to land, equipment and credit
8 Legal rights and political power
9 Violence against women
10 Macroeconomic policy and gender

These areas cover some of the most important indicators to be collected at the national level.[1] The following tables are indicative or a checklist, in that they provide broad guidelines within which specific indicators should be generated. The tables should be adapted for use by governments depending on the local context.

In addition to suggesting indicators, the tables also provide related indicator questions which deal with broader socio-economic questions related to the topic and to gender relations at the national level. The first column of the tables includes basic indicators which should be collected routinely in order to develop a basic database on questions of gender equity. The indicator questions complement the indicators by asking the kinds of questions that are usually addressed during gender analysis. Dealing with broader socioeconomic areas, these questions ask why the situation that the indicator describes has come about, what it tells us about gender relations, and how this situation can be changed.

Population Composition and Change[2]

Indicators of population composition and change are important in determining the process of social and economic development in a country and hence for the planning of development policies. All such data should be collected on a sex-disaggregated basis. Collection and use of population composition indicators can assist with the prediction of the potential demand for and use of social and other services in a gendered fashion. Population composition and change data is usually available from the national census and special studies.

Table 1   **Population Composition and Change**

Gender-Sensitive Indicator	Related Indicator Questions
1 Size of the population by sex, total and % under 15	✦ What is the sex ratio in the country? Is there a reverse sex ratio? Does this vary by region?
2 Sex ratio (number of females to males)	✦ If there is a reverse sex ratio, what are the reasons for this? What are the means of changing this situation and how can women and men be involved in these changes?
3 Births and deaths by sex (numbers and rates per 1,000), annually	
4 Net international migration rates by sex	✦ Does international and internal migration vary by sex? If this is the case, what are the reasons for this variation?
5 Net internal migration rates by sex	✦ Do migration patterns at regional and national levels adversely affect women? If this is the case, how can this situation change and what input can women and men make to these changes?

Two of the most important sets of indicators under this heading relate to the sex ratio and migration. The 'normal' sex ratio is approximately 1:1, or one woman to one man. However, economists using population composition data from national censuses have shown that in some parts of Asia the sex ratio is strongly biased against women (Dreze and Sen, 1989). The sex ratio is therefore a useful diagnostic indicator which can point to gender biases in a given country, and the reasons for these biases can be explored using gender analysis.

Migration is important in terms of gender because of the impact that both internal and international migration can have on the household, and because of opportunities that migration can offer to women. This impact is felt both when men migrate and women continue to work in the household, and when women themselves choose to migrate. Migrant women in particular are often a disadvantaged group as they usually have little education or socially valued job skills, and have to adjust to a new environment.

Table 2   Human Settlements and Geographical Distribution

Gender-Sensitive Indicator	Related Indicator Questions
1 Number, % distribution and density of population by sex, geographical area and urban/rural	✦ Is there a pattern of concentration of women and men in particular regions or in urban or rural areas as a result of migration or other factors? If so, does this impact negatively on women? Is there discrimination against rural women and if so, what policies can be implemented to reverse this situation?
2 Degree of discrimination against rural women: Rural and urban mortality rates, life expectancy and nutritional status	
3 Stock and characteristics of housing (materials used in construction of outer walls, floors and roofs; number of rooms; kitchen and bathroom facilities; availability of water and bathroom facilities), by region and by female- and male-headed households	✦ Do the characteristics of housing differ by male- and female-headed household? Are living conditions worse for female-headed households, and by what degree? How can policy improve this situation? ✦ Are there constitutional, legal or administrative impediments to women's access to and ownership of land and housing?
4 Tenure of household, by region and by female- and male-headed households	✦ Is there gender bias between different kinds of households concerning energy consumption? If so, how does this affect women? How can policy improve the situation?
5 Domestic household energy consumption by region and by female- and male-headed households	
6 Time-use in connection with household activities (collection of water, fuel, food), by region and by female and male headed households	✦ Are women spending more time on household-related activities than men? If so, what are the implications for gender relations within the household and how can these relations be made more equal by policy intervention?

Human Settlements and Geographical Distribution

Serious concerns have been expressed about the conditions in which women are living. The generation of socioeconomic and demographic indicators by geographical area can be used to differentiate between living conditions in specified areas and to develop policies for reducing disparities. Indicators of housing conditions and facilities available to households reveal where poor housing conditions impact most heavily on women as the main providers of reproductive labour.

Human settlements and geographical distribution indicators are among the indicators least amenable to differentiation by sex. One means of making them more gender-sensitive is to disaggregate data by female and male heads of household, so as to establish if female-headed households are discriminated against in terms of housing conditions and access to facilities.

One key element of CEDAW is to report on discrimination against rural women, and collecting data on geographical distribution will enable such reporting. Much of the information on human settlements and geographical distribution is available in population censuses and from time-use surveys.

Households and Families, Marital Status, Fertility

The position of women within the household or family is often a key element in relation to gender inequality and to women's participation in society as a whole. Defining the household or family in such as way as to allow for the variety of living arrangements is complex, but flexible definitions of household and family will facilitate a greater understanding of women's role as well as the distribution of intra-household resources. It is particularly important to define the concept of 'household head' in a fashion which recognises the role played by many women as main household provider, whether women or men are registered as the household head in censuses and other surveys.

The main sources of data in this area are censuses and demographic surveys.

Table 3 **Households and Families, Marital Status, Fertility**

Gender-Sensitive Indicator	Related Indicator Questions
1 Number and % distribution of households	✦ How is household head defined? Is the definition broad enough to include women's role within the household?
2 % distribution of population in households by size	✦ What is the significance of the extent of male/female heads of household? Are more female-headed households poor, and if so, what are the reasons for this?
3 % of households headed by women/men	
4 % of poor households headed by women/men	✦ Do women and men living in the same household as a married couple or otherwise have the same rights and responsibilities?
5 Crude birth rate, per 1,000 women in specified age group[3]	✦ Is divorce available to men and women on the same grounds?
	✦ How are household decisions made concerning the number and spacing of children?

Learning in Formal and Non-Formal Education

Education indicators are among the most important for measuring the status of women and gender equity, and one of the better reported areas, mainly in censuses and administrative records. Educational indicators can also be found in UNESCO's *Statistical Yearbooks*. Several international studies have focused on the key role of the education of the girl-child and women in improving women's status (World Bank, 1995b).

Two main categories of education indicators have been distinguished. The first relates to indicators of educational characteristics of the population, including literacy, educational attainment, access to education and school attendance. The second relates to indicators of the educational system, including enrolment, retention, educational resources and curricula.

There are differing views as to which indicators best reflect gender inequity. The use of gender-sensitive indicators involves trade-offs of various kinds, for example between accuracy of data and relevance to women. Enrolment rates, which, along with literacy, are among the education indicators most commonly used to measure the status of women, are a good example of this.[4]

Table 4   Education

Gender-Sensitive Indicator	Related Indicator Questions
1 Numbers and percentages of literate persons, by sex and age	✦ Is there equal access to education in practice? If not, which factors cause differential access to education by women and men? If there is discrimination, how can this be changed and how can women and men take part in this process of change?
2 Years of schooling completed, by level and sex	
3 Access to specialised training programmes (vocational, technical and professional) at the secondary level and above, by sex	✦ What uses do women and men make of their education? Does the social context allow women to make full use of their education?
4 % of women/men graduating in the fields of law/sciences/medicine	✦ Do women and men enrol in university subjects according to gender stereotypes? Can the government intervene to challenge such gender stereotyping?
5 Gross primary and secondary school enrolment ratio for girls/boys	✦ Are women and men stereotyped in school curricula? How can these curricula be changed to eliminate gender stereotyping and present in a positive light women, men and gender relations?
6 Enrolment ratios of women and men in tertiary education and university	
7 Female/male dropout rates at primary, secondary and tertiary levels	✦ Have legislative or other measures been taken to ensure equal access to education for women and men?
8 % of female/male teachers at primary, secondary and tertiary levels	
9 % of female/male school principals and university heads of departments	

The standard enrolment indicator, *the number of children enrolled in primary or secondary school as a percentage of total number of children in the relevant age group for that level*, otherwise known as 'gross enrolment', is problematic because it assumes an orderly and simple relationship between age group and level of education. "In many countries, the figures for primary school enrolment in fact reach more than 100 per cent, because many children of secondary school age attend primary school" (Anderson, 1991: 56). Anderson suggests instead as an indicator *net enrolment ratios showing the total number of children enrolled in a schooling level who belong to the relevant age group, expressed as a percentage of the total number of children in that age group*, otherwise known as 'net enrolment'.

Anderson also suggests that the net enrolment ratio for primary schools is the most suitable educational indicator, as secondary school net enrolment ratios may reflect whether or not a country has a compulsory stage of secondary education (1991: 56).

One problem with net enrolment ratios is that data for them may be less readily accessible than for gross enrolment rates. In addition:

"Although enrolment rates may be associated with literacy levels among girls and may be used as current bench-marks so that future progress may be measured, enrolment at the elementary level is not the most significant figure. In societies where parents feel it is important to invest in the education of boys but not girls, it is likely that few girls will attain secondary levels of education, let alone a university education. Thus, it is important to obtain not only enrolment statistics, but to obtain enrolment statistics by level, and, at the higher levels, by the field of study, which may indicate the different types of educational pyramids which exist for girls and boys and also the changes in the shape of the pyramids over time."

UN, 1984a: 35

The trade-off involved in choosing one or the other of the indicators is illustrated in Figure 1, which puts the indicators into high or low categories. It is apparent that there is no perfect indicator to measure gendered enrolment.

Figure 1   **Strengths and Weaknesses of Educational Indicators from a Gender Perspective**

Indicator	Relevance to Women	Availability of Data	Precision of Measurement
Gross enrolment at primary level	Low	High	Low
Gross enrolment at secondary level	High	High	Low
Net enrolment at primary level	Low	Low	High
Net enrolment at secondary level	High	Low	High

There are three further points to make about enrolment ratios:

1 Enrolment ratios reveal how many people enrol but not how many attend. "Because censuses do not provide data which permit an examination of absences and drop-outs, except by inference over long periods, it is important to supplement census data with other material which will provide information on this pattern of attendance" (UN, 1984a: 35). However, data on dropout rates for developing countries is not readily accessible.

2 Enrolment ratios do not cover the qualitative area of the make-up of the curriculum. "Even when girls are attending school, they may be experiencing a very different type of educational training than are boys. In many societies the curriculum deemed appropriate for girls may be totally unrelated to potential later employment" (UN, 1984a: 36). A key area is gender stereotyping within school and university curricula. This is a complex area, difficult to narrow down into specific indicators. School and university curricula should be examined through the use of special studies and surveys to determine their gender content.

3 Enrolment ratios are indicators of process rather than of outcome. Outcome indicators can be literacy rates, and these are usually considered more significant than enrolment ratios because they represent the outcome of schooling. However, there is also a trade off in choice of indicators of literacy. Basic literacy rates, as defined by UNESCO, measure the ability to both read and write a short simple statement on one's everyday life. Some documents (e.g., UN, 1989) suggest that functional literacy (i.e., the ability to read a newspaper) is a better outcome indicator; however, functional literacy rates are not usually collected for developing countries.

There are also constraints with use of literacy as an indicator. Literacy reflects the functioning of the education system over a number of years. "The average age of the developing world population over 15 is 36, therefore adult education measures reflect the average social effort for education about 20 to 35 years ago ... Such prevalence measures are relatively insensitive to the current social investment in educating youth" (Murray, 1993: 46).

Health, Health Services, Nutrition

Indicators of health are particularly important for the determination of changes in women's status over time. Health indicators should be carefully selected. Indicators on health services and health conditions are weak in most developing countries. Health indicators tend to be found in administrative records and special surveys. The following are key areas where data should be collected (UN, 1990):

✦ the state of health of the population;
✦ availability and accessibility of resources;
✦ use of health resources (hospitals, etc.);
✦ environmental data (e.g. related to pollution); and
✦ outcomes of preventive and curative measures.

Life expectancy and infant mortality are two indirect health indicators most commonly used for the measurement of the status of women.

Gender-sensitive health indicators do present a number of methodological problems.[5] Life expectancy at birth, for example, may be problematic because whether or not a person dies in a given year depends on factors over their whole lives and may not reflect present circumstances.

"Whether someone who is 70 years old will survive to 71 or not depends on a large set of factors over the whole of their lives. There is therefore a built-in time-lag, of the order of 35 years, between cause and effect ....The only way round this problem ... is to take the shortest gap between death and birth, which must be the youngest age group ....This information is provided by the infant mortality rate, which is defined as the number of deaths under one year of age during a year, per thousand live births during that year."

Anderson, 1991: 62

The infant mortality rate reflects infants' and mothers' health, environmental health, and general socioeconomic development, and is closely related to literacy. However, the infant mortality rate, like all indicators, presents problems. Accurate infant mortality data may not be available; for example, nearly every African county has data on the number of hospital beds, but "hardly have any complete and reliable infant mortality rates" (McGranahan *et al*, 1985: 9). Also, the infant mortality rate may be a poor predictor of life expectancy: "With the widespread application in developing countries of health technologies targeted to infants and children ... the link between child mortality and mortality at other ages has been further weakened" (Murray, 1993: 42).

Table 5   **Health, Health Services, Nutrition**

Gender-Sensitive Indicator	Related Indicator Questions
1 % of government expenditure devoted to women's health needs in a) productive and b) non-productive areas	✦ Are women and girls discriminated against in terms of access to health care? If so, what are the reasons for this and how can this discrimination be overcome?
2 Number of/access to primary health care centres by sex	✦ What % of health personnel are women, at the different levels of the health system?
3 Number of visits to and number of bed-nights spent in hospital by women/men; number of hospital beds as % of population	✦ If mortality and morbidity rates differ between men and women, what is the reason for this? What are the major causes of infant and child morbidity in girls and boys?
4 Proportion of girls and boys immunised against specific diseases	✦ What cultural and other obstacles are there to women and girls receiving health care and family planning services?
5 Proportion of births attended by a physician, midwife or trained auxiliary	✦ Is abortion legal, and if so, are services available in practice?
6 Mortality and length of life, by sex	✦ Have any programmes been introduced to combat AIDS, and have any of these programmes been developed with a focus on women?
7 Maternal mortality rates (per 1,000 live births)	✦ Is intra-household distribution of food biased against women and girls? If so, what are the reasons for this?
8 Infant mortality rates and female/male ratio	✦ Do women spend more on food than men? If so, what are the implications of this?
9 Number and/or incidence of selected communicable diseases of public health importance, including AIDS, by sex	✦ Does access to sanitation and clean water differ by sex? If so, what are the implications of this for women's health?
10 Calorie consumption as a % of minimum requirements, by sex	
11 % of women's/men's incomes spent on food	
12 Access to sanitation and clean water, by sex	

Economic Activity and Labour Force Participation

Measurement of economic activity and labour force participation is a complex but key area for the advancement of women's status and gender equality and equity. It is generally agreed that women's economic activity is under-represented in most censuses and national level surveys, and that the contribution of women to economic development is an area where lack of data is most acute. The following gender-sensitive indicators and indicator questions are designed to allow the user to develop a basic data set on women and economic activity.

There are two key areas to be considered in the formation of a national level data base on women. The first is the inclusion of gender-sensitive questions that are fully understood by all participating, including enumerators, in censuses and similar surveys. The second is a reconsideration of the concepts used in the UN System of National Accounts (SNA) as far as work is concerned.

Definitions of economic activity

Economic activity is perhaps the most difficult of the concepts used in censuses. The generally used term 'economically active population' is problematic because it represents a number of disparate components. The main work-related categories are:

+ **activity status** (currently active, usually active, and economically active sometime during the year);
+ **employment status** (employed, unemployed, not economically active);
+ **employment characteristics** (occupation, industry, status in employment, and sector of employment);
+ **duration of employment** (hours worked last week, weeks worked last year).

As UN (1993) states, the term 'economically active population' "… combines the employed with the unemployed population; full time with part-time activity; the activity of the worker who is paid for one hour's work in a specified reference period with that of another working full-time throughout the same period; seasonal activities in some instances and current or usual activities in others". However, advances have been made over the last 15 years particularly in the improvement of definitions of terminology related to economic activity.

The focus of SNA and ILO definitions of work relate to economic activity. But 'economic activity' is often defined in an unclear or ambiguous fashion (Anker et al, 1988). For example, according to the

Table 6   Economic Activity and Labour Force Participation

Gender-Sensitive Indicator	Related Indicator Questions
1 % of female/male labour force in agriculture, industry and services (ages 15 and over)	✦ Are there areas where men or women predominantly work? Does sex-stereotyping in employment exist? If so, what are the consequences of this?
2 % of female/male labour force in managerial and professional occupations	✦ What provisions exist to eliminate discrimination against women in employment? How are these provisions enforced?
3 % of female/male labour force who are unpaid family workers or are working in the informal sector (ages 15 and over)	✦ Are women moving to better or worse paid employment? What are the consequences of this for women?
4 Employment/unemployment rate of women/men, urban/rural	✦ Are there professions which, by law or custom, tend to be filled predominantly by or are closed to women?
5 Time use in selected activities (including unpaid housework and child care)	✦ Is there a bias against women in terms of employment because of a lack of child-care facilities?
6 Incidence of part time/full time work of women and men	✦ Do women receive equal pay as men for equal work or work of equal value?
7 Right to maternity leave/number of weeks/% of women who avail of right	✦ What legislation exists to ensure women's equality in terms of employment? How is this legislation enforced in practice?
8 % of available credit and financial and technical support going to women/men from government and non-government sources	✦ Is work done by women in the home counted in national statistics? Do national statistics reflect the role of women in the economic sector? What means are being taken to ensure that censuses and other surveys accurately reflect the economic role of women within and outside of the household?
9 Salary/wage differentials of women/men, by class of workers	
10 % of employers providing child care and % of children aged 0-3 and 3-6 in child care	

SNA, processing of food for preservation, husking of rice and grinding of grain are considered economic activities, while cooking is not, but the dividing line between these activities is a very thin one. Anker *et al* (1988) point out several similar anomalies, and in response suggest a useful four-part typology to measure labour force activity:

+ paid labour force, that is persons in wage or salary employment for which they are paid in cash or kind;
+ market-oriented labour force, that is persons in 'paid labour force' plus persons engaged in an activity on a family farm or in a family enterprise that sells some or all of its products;
+ ILO labour force, that is persons engaged in the production of economic goods and services, whether these goods and services are sold or not. This includes all activities associated with primary products, such as food production and food processing;
+ extended labour force, including all of the above and activities such as gathering and preparing fuel and water fetching.

This typology is useful in that it extends the definition in the SNA and covers many of the activities carried out by women. Unpaid work such as housework and child-care are not included.

Unpaid work and the System of National Accounts

As a tool for economic policy-making, the SNA is a key area where governments can improve the way in which gender-disaggregated data is collected and used.

With a concentration on measuring paid employment, measures such as the SNA and GDP have been heavily criticised for their gender bias, in particular ignoring women's contribution to the economy, and to society as a whole.

There has over the last ten years been extensive methodological debate related to the valuation of unpaid work, in particular in relation to definitions of different kinds of unpaid work and imputation of value (e.g. through replacement or opportunity costs, or both).[6] This guide focuses on specific gender-sensitive indicators that could be employed in parallel to the SNA.

The 1993 SNA divides unpaid work into three types:

1   Housework, child care and other family-related services (mainly carried out by women), which are not recognised by SNA as economic activity.

2 Subsistence and non-market activities such as agricultural production for household consumption (much of which is carried out by women), to be valued in the SNA from 1993 on the basis of market values of similar services that are sold.

3 Household enterprises producing for the market for which more than one household member provides unpaid labour. The income and production of these enterprises are quantified in SNA using transaction values.

Much of the recent discussion about unpaid housework including child-care, caring for dependants and providing voluntary services, has been in relation to developing a parallel or satellite account to the SNA. The World Summit on Social Development in Copenhagen noted: "Efforts are needed to acknowledge the social and economic importance and value of unremunerated work … including by developing methods for reflecting its value … in accounts that may be produced separately from, but consistent with core national accounts" (UN, 1995a: para 46). Similar recommendations can be found in the Beijing Platform for Action.

The 1993 SNA gives detailed instructions for the setting up of satellite accounts, which should be developed in the same way as main accounts (Inter-Secretariat Working Group, 1993). However, the sections on satellite accounts in the SNA do not provide examples related to unpaid work.

Several OECD countries have developed satellite accounts in relation to unpaid housework. Other countries are developing national time-use surveys: "Most of these countries have used or will use these data to produce estimates of household work or of total unpaid work, or … to establish a satellite account for the household sector, including household production, or … to develop an input-output table for the non-market household sphere" (Chadeau, 1993: 66). Although it is recognised that there is a need to harmonise approaches to allow international comparison, it is also recognised that because of methodological disputes and data differences between countries, some flexibility is required (Statistics Canada, 1993).

There is some agreement that the first step in terms of measuring unpaid housework and related aspects of unpaid work is to measure the amount of time spent on these activities. This is the approach taken, for example, in questions on unpaid work in the 1996 Canadian census. Once the time spent on activities is calculated a value can be given to this time. Time-use studies are thus particularly important for this area of the development of gender-sensitive indicators.

There is also some consensus as to what is to be included as important unpaid work, even if not as to how to estimate its value. The key areas are:

+ domestic work, including meal preparation, cleaning up after food or meal preparation; cleaning inside and outside the house; clothing care, including laundry, ironing and clothes and shoe repair; and repairs and maintenance, including home repairs, gardening and grounds maintenance;

+ help and child care, including physical care of children, education and medical care of children; and adult care, including personal and medical care; management and shopping including household administration and shopping for goods and services;

+ transportation and travel;

+ volunteer work, including fundraising, attending meetings and research;

+ unpaid work in the labour force.

Specific indicators, as illustrative examples related to domestic work that could be included in national time-use studies, are as follows. An example of a straightforward question would be (taken from 1996 Canadian census): "Number of hours per week spent by household members doing unpaid housework, yard work or home maintenance for members of this household, or others". Alternatively, this question could be asked in the following way:

"Now let's talk about housework, including cooking and cleaning and doing other work around the house:
1   Do you prepare food for meals or wash dishes?
2   Do you do grocery shopping?
3   Do you clean and vacuum?
4   Do you do laundry?
5   Do you sew and mend?
Altogether, about how many hours do you spend doing these things in an average week?"
Statistics Canada, 1993: 117

Similar lines of enquiry could be pursued for other areas of unpaid work, with all data sex-disaggregated to determine women and men's contributions. The next stage would be to place a value on each of these areas of unpaid work so that satellite national accounts can be developed.

As discussion on the valuation and importance of unpaid work becomes more sophisticated, the development of satellite accounts related to unpaid work through time-use and other studies offers an opportunity for governments to make significant progress. However, "very few time-use surveys have been conducted at the national level in developing countries" (Harvey, 1993). So the first step would be to design national level time-use studies concentrating on unpaid work and to experiment with different forms of imputation of value for this work. INSTRAW has been co-ordinating a number of studies in this area in developing countries (Harvey, 1993).

Access to Land, Equipment and Credit

Women's land ownership rights differ from country to country, but it is clear that generally land is under male ownership and control. There has been little systematic focus on the question on women's access to and control over land, despite the potential importance of land to the improvement of women's status and gender equity. While in law women have the right to own land in South Asia, in practice women's ownership and control is rare (Agarwal, 1994: 468). Key questions in this area therefore include whether legislation exists at the country level that ensures gender equality in both access to and control over land.

The World Conference on Agrarian Reform and Rural Development (WCARRD), which requires member countries of the FAO to report on various aspects of agrarian development, has suggested indicators for access to land, water and other natural resources (Dey-Abbas and Gaiha, 1993: 250-1).

States Parties of CEDAW are required to report on Article 14 on discrimination against rural women, Section (g) of which states that women have the right: "to have access to agricultural credit and loans, marketing facilities, appropriate technology and equal treatment in land and agrarian reform as well as in land resettlement schemes".

Some gender-sensitive indicators may be available from agricultural censuses, or such censuses could be adapted to ensure that gender-sensitive indicators are included.

An important differentiation between indicators of access and control over rural resources occurs in the case of credit. In one of the best known cases of women's access to credit, the Grameen Bank in Bangladesh, there is evidence that while loans are made to and have to be repaid by women, it may be men who made key decisions over how the loan is used (Goetz and Sen Gupta, 1996). This highlights the importance of using indicators in combination with qualitative analysis such as the related questions given in the tables. To stop at the use of gender-sensitive indicators in this case would have shown greater gender equality, but analysis of intra-household decision-making may have revealed a more complex pattern of gender discrimination.

Table 7   **Access to Land, Equipment and Credit**

Gender-Sensitive Indicator	Related Indicator Questions
1 % of property owned or accessible by women (land, houses, livestock), across income groups	✦ Is land mainly under the control of men or women? What are the consequences of this for gender relations, decisions about land sales and cropping patterns?
2 % of women who have access to credit, vis-à-vis men	✦ What are the inheritance practices in the country concerning land? If women can legally inherit land, do they do this in practice?
3 % of rural households where female/male head is the main household earner	✦ If women own land does this also mean that they make decisions concerning crop selection and marketing?
4 % of female/male headed households without land	✦ Has land reform benefited men and women equally?
5 % average wage rates for agricultural labourers, by sex	✦ Do women have equal access to credit facilities: Does such access translate into control over credit in terms of decision-making?
6 % of women/men who have received land titles under land reform schemes	✦ Is there a difference between women and men's agricultural labour wages?

Legal Rights and Political Power [7]

There has been increasing focus on women's legal rights and political power over the last ten years, a focus that work on indicators is only beginning to reflect. However, a number of indicators can be extrapolated from the literature related to this area. For example the UNDP Gender Empowerment Matrix employs as one of its indicators the commonly used "share of parliamentary seats going to women and men". *The World's Women* (UN, 1995a) uses as indicators: "Countries where more than 15%

Table 8   **Political and Public Life**

Gender-Sensitive Indicator	Related Indicator Questions
1 % of seats held by women and men in national parliaments and local government/decision-making bodies	✦ What are the obstacles that prevent women from gaining decision-making positions in government or the civil service?
2 % of women and men in decision-making positions in government	✦ What are the obstacles that prevent women from gaining decision-making positions in the judicial system and the police force?
3 % of women and men electoral candidates/officers in political parties	✦ Do courts or other tribunals promote and protect the rights of women?
4 % of women in the civil service, at four highest levels of office	✦ Is one socio-economic group dominant as far as holding decision-making positions is concerned?
5 % of women employed in the public sector, at administrative and managerial levels	✦ How many cases of gender discrimination were brought before the courts or other government bodies in the last four years? How were they decided?
6 % of women/men registered as voters/% of eligible women/men who vote	✦ What input do women make to changes in the political system?
7 % of women in senior/junior decision-making positions within unions	
8 % of women judges, justices and prosecutors	
9 % of women in the police force, by rank	

of ministers or subministers are women", "% of women in decision-making positions in government by field", and "women in broadcasting and the press". A number of similar indicators could be employed, dependent on data availability, but again with the caveat that indicators will only paint the broad picture of women's and men's participation.

Indicators of empowerment and participation in CEDAW reporting

Reporting requirements under CEDAW often result in the first comprehensive review of the situation of women in a particular country (CEDAW, 1995). But CEDAW is also a key convention because it requires reporting on cultural, legal and political areas which are not covered in any of the standard mechanisms from which gender-sensitive indicators can be taken, for example censuses. These areas are:
+ sex roles and stereotyping (Article 5);
+ suppression of the exploitation of women (Article 6);
+ political and public life (Article 7);
+ international representation and participation (Article 8);
+ equality before the law and in civil matters (Article 15);
+ equality in marriage and family law (Article 16).

In addition, General Recommendations 12 and 14 of CEDAW require states parties to include information relating to all forms of violence against women, including female circumcision. As such the Convention reflects recent changes in understanding as to the means by which to progress towards gender equality, and in particular a focus on women's rights (CEDAW, 1995b). CEDAW requires not only the listing of laws related to gender equality but also statistical reporting on the effects of implementation of these laws.

However, the reports of states parties are often weak in areas relating to women's rights, empowerment and participation. While the reports may contain extensive documentation and indicators relating to health and education, the sections relating to, for example, Articles 5 and 7 are often quite short.

Overall, CEDAW is an excellent mechanism for collecting gender-sensitive data in areas such as empowerment, participation and violence not covered in many other national level surveys. Such data will need to be generated from specially commissioned surveys.

Violence against Women

As with political power, there has also been increasing attention paid in the last ten years to violence against women. Discussion of violence against women is also included in the focus on women's rights as human rights (Amnesty International, 1995). *The World's Women* notes:

"Currently the only quantitative data that most governments collect on violence against women are reported crime statistics on rape, assault and various other sexual crimes. These have serious limitations and should be complemented with data from other sources. Questions related to intimate assault and rape can be added to population-based surveys... or crime victimisation surveys ... Experience has shown that disclosure of violence is greatly influenced by the content of the questions, (and) the context of the questioning ... questions and questionnaires must be carefully planned and interviewers carefully selected and trained to ask direct questions about violence."

UN, 1995a: 164

The World's Women (UN 1995a) uses, among others, as key indicators:

+ % of adult women who have been physically assaulted by an intimate partner;
+ % of women in selected large cities who were sexually assaulted in a five-year period;
+ numbers of NGOs working on violence against women;
+ rape reform laws passed;
+ domestic violence reforms passed;
+ government body responsible for anti-violence programming.

Table 9 contains gender-sensitive indicators in the key area of violence against women. These indicators will need to be generated through the use of specially commissioned surveys.

Macroeconomic Policy and Gender

The final priority area to be covered here is macro-economic policy and gender. Integrating gender into national budgetary processes has become an important focus for many countries. This can be done in particular by examining national budgets for gender-

Table 9   Indicators of Gender-Related Violence

Gender-Sensitive Indicator	Related Indicator Questions
1 Number of reported cases of domestic violence	✦ Has the country followed CEDAW recommendations and reported on laws enacted to protect women from violence?
2 Number of reported cases of sexual assault and rape	✦ How effective is legislation banning different forms of violence against women?
3 Number of reported cases of sexual harassment	✦ Are the representations of women in the media, in advertising or in school curricula likely to lead to violence against women?
4 Conviction rates of accused violent offenders against women	✦ In what ways have women organised to combat violence? What has been the result of this organisation?
5 Number of immediate protective measures taken to assist abused women (legal aid, financial assistance, housing assistance, shelters, police action, NGO efforts)	✦ Does the country enforce the UN Convention prohibiting the slave trade and exploitation through prostitution? What measures does the country have to address the commercial sexual exploitation of the girl-child?
6 Increase/decrease of violence against women during armed conflict	✦ Are women refugees protected during periods of armed conflict?

sensitivity and estimating budgetary expenditure going towards priority areas as they affect women and men.

The Commonwealth Secretariat is developing a series of policy options for integrating gender into national budgetary policies in the context of economic reform. The policy options centre on six possible tools :

✦ **sex-disaggregated beneficiary assessments** – a research technique whereby groups of women are asked how, if they were the Finance Minister, they would slice the national budgetary pie; the results are compared with the existing budget to see how closely it reflects women's priorities;

✦ **sex-disaggregated public expenditure incidence analysis** – this involves analysing public expenditures in such areas as health, education and agriculture to see how such expenditures benefit women and men, girls and boys to differing degrees;

✦ **gender-aware policy evaluation of public expenditure** – evaluating the policy assumptions that underlie budgetary appropriations, to identify their likely impact on current patterns and degrees of gender differences;

✦ **gender-aware budget statement** – a modification of the Women's Budget; this is a statement from each sectoral ministry or line department on the gender implications of the budget within that sector;

✦ **sex-disaggregated analysis of the impact of the budget on time-use** – this looks at the relationship between the national budget and the way time is used in households, so as to reveal the macroeconomic implications of unpaid work such as caring for the family, the sick and community members, collecting fuel and water, cooking, cleaning, teaching children and so on;

✦ **gender-aware medium-term economic policy framework** – medium-term macroeconomic policy frameworks are currently formulated using a variety of economy-wide models which are usually 'gender-blind'. Approaches for integrating gender could include: disaggregating variables by gender where applicable; introducing new variables incorporating a gender perspective; constructing new models that incorporate both national income accounts and household income accounts reflecting unpaid work; and changing underlying assumptions about the social and institutional set-up for economic planning.

At present, indicators in the area of national level budgeting are patchy and usually not internationally comparable. The indicators given in Table 10 are therefore illustrative of key areas where governments should refine budgetary planning to ensure that gender-sensitive data is available. Some areas of national level budgetary expenditure have already been covered in Tables 4 and 5, and other relevant discussion of national level accounts and labour force activity can be found in the discussion of the System of National Accounts in Section 2.

Table 10   Macroeconomic Policy and Gender

Gender-Sensitive Indicator	Related Indicator Questions
1 Private consumption expenditure of households	✦ How much of the household's expenditure is directed towards the purchase of food, and education and health related matters? Who controls the household budget, and what say do women have in expenditure?
2 Total government expenditure and as percentage of GDP	
3 Breakdown of government expenditure by sector	✦ How far is government expenditure directed towards priority areas for women such as education and health? What role do women have in national level budgetary planning?
4 Proportion of persons and households at risk covered by social security and similar schemes	✦ Are health and education systems privatised and if so, what are the gender implications of this?
5 Proportion of potentially eligible persons and households receiving social insurance, social assistance and similar benefits	✦ Are women adequately covered by social security and other schemes? Are such schemes sufficiently gender-sensitive? Is sufficient attention being paid during national level budgetary planning to groups at risk, such as poor single mothers and female headed households?

Notes

1 These areas have been identified as international priorities in UN recommendations (UN 1995b; 1990a; 1989; UNDP, 1995) and the Beijing Platform for Action (1995). The material in this section also draws from CIDA (1996a) and Commonwealth Secretariat (1996). UN (1990) also provides listings of indicators under each of these classifications.

2 Sections 3.1-3.3 are drawn from UN (1990a; 1989).

3 The crude birth rate is obtained by dividing the average number of women of childbearing age in the population in one year, by the number of live births occurring during the same period.

4 The following section is adapted from CIDA (1996a; 1996b) and UN (1990a).

5 The following section is adapted from CIDA (1996a; 1996b) and UN (1990a).

6 Much of this debate is summarised in Statistics Canada (1995b; 1993) and Goldschmidt-Clermont (1987).

7 This and the following section draw on CIDA (1996a; 1996b).

4 Gender-Sensitive Indicators: The State of the Art[1]

Extensive work has been undertaken in the last five to ten years on indicators at the national level. This section reviews some of the main work specifically on gender-sensitive indicators that have been carried out by the UN and donors.

UNDP 1995 Human Development Report

Since 1990 the UNDP has produced an influential *Human Development Report* which has included a discussion of development related issues and a composite index of human development, the Human Development Index (HDI). This composite index is made up of three areas: purchasing power parity, adult literacy and years of schooling, and life expectancy. While there have been a number of criticisms of the HDI, mainly related to technical aspects of indicator use and the HDIs conceptual underpinnings, the *Human Development Report* is at present the most widely quoted and widely used report on indicators at the national and regional levels.

In preparation for the 1995 UN World Conference on Women, the 1995 UNDP Human Development Report focused on gender, by introducing two composite indexes to measure gender equity (the GDI) and women's empowerment (the GEM). These two composite indexes are likely to be very important indexes in future discussions on the measurement of gender inequality and gendered country level planning, and deserve the attention of governments.

Gender-related development index (GDI)

The GDI utilises country level achievements in the same areas as the HDI, that is income, education and life expectancy. The greater the gender disparity within a country in these areas, the lower a country's GDI becomes as compared to its HDI. The reference group in this index and the GEM is men. The methodology used for the GDI imposes a penalty for inequality, so that the GDI achievement of a country falls when the achievement levels of both women and men in a country go down, or when the disparity between their achievements increases. Calculation of the GDI involves the use of complex econometric techniques which may hinder the widespread use and understanding of such indexes. The GDI was developed to show that no society treats its women as well as its men and that gender equality does not depend on the income level in a society.

The GDI is a useful methodological tool which can capture changes in gender relations over time both within a country and between countries, as measured by a small number of important indicators of the quality of life.

Gender empowerment measure (GEM)

The GEM examines whether women and men are able to participate actively in economic and political life. To do so, it uses easily accessible data to measure 'empowerment' in the spheres of economic and political participation. It uses three indicators:
+ per capita income in purchasing power parity in US dollars;
+ the share of jobs classified as professional and technical, and administrative and managerial, going to men and women;
+ the share of parliamentary seats going to women and men.

The three dimensions of empowerment are valued equally in the measure, and as with the GDI a complex econometric analysis is performed to determine the GEM for the 116 countries for which data is considered reliable.

The *Human Development Report* draws various conclusions by comparing the GEM and HDI, the GEM and GDI, and the GEM and income per capita. Such comparisons are useful for countries to make in order to determine how progressive countries are in achieving gender equality. Among the findings which can be extrapolated are:

Some developing countries outperform much richer industrial countries in gender equality in political, economic and professional activities.
+ Some countries have low GEM values as compared to their GDI ranking, which means that they are achieving more in

terms of education and literacy than in terms of employment and political participation.

✦ Several countries in East and South East Asia that have followed an East Asian development model have low GEM values, pointing to the marginal participation of women at political, economic and managerial decision-making levels, despite high economic growth.

Limitations of the GDI and GEM

Countries could attempt to improve gender-related reporting by using composite indexes such as those in the *Human Development Report*. But if they are to be used it should be recognised that both the GDI and GEM have some limitations:

✦ **Choice of indicators:** As in all composite indexes the choice of indicators is to a certain extent arbitrary. For example, if the GEM had chosen as one of its indicators 'membership of unions', rankings would also have been quite different.

✦ **Weighting of indicators:** This is a problem with all composite indexes, as there is no objective reason why, for example, education should be weighted equally with life expectancy.

✦ **Lack of participation in indicator choice:** The GDI and GEM, as well as the HDI, have been developed with very little public participation, with indicators chosen by specialists. In addition, the calculation of the GDI and GEM can be understood only by specialists because of the complexity of the calculations involved, making it difficult to facilitate public participation.

UN Publications

The World's Women 1995: Trends and Statistics. UN (1995a):

This is probably the most comprehensive source of data on the situation and status of women at the national level. It was developed from the UN *Women's Indicators and Statistics Database* (WISTAT) which is taken mainly from official national sources, such as national population and housing censuses and household sample surveys. It covers five main areas: population; health; education and training; work; and power, influence and violence against women. Its comprehensive nature and sectoral organisation makes this document a very useful guide for governments looking to summarise data concerning gender at the national level. Some gaps remain, however, particularly regarding availability and reliability of data.

Gender Indicators of Developing Asian and Pacific Countries, Manila: Asian Development Bank, 1993:

This document was produced by the Centre for International Research of the US Bureau of the Census, with the aim of grouping and disseminating statistics that were scattered among sectoral statistics and publications. Indicators are organised by sector and by country, and include:

+ population size and age characteristics, including sex ratios by age;
+ fertility, mortality, and population change, including crude birth and death rates, maternal mortality at delivery, and infant mortality rates;
+ contraceptive use;
+ marriage and households, including average household size and women heads of households;
+ literacy and education, including literacy rates by age and enrolment rates;
+ labour force participation, including labour force distribution of employment and unpaid female employment.

FAO's socioeconomic indicator programme following from the World Conference on Agrarian Reform and Rural Development (WCARRD)

At the 1979 WCARRD, FAO member countries agreed to collect on a regular basis quantitative data on a range of indicators pertinent to agrarian reform and rural development. Ensuring that these country reports are prepared on a regular basis and contain relevant gender-disaggregated data would be one means of identifying relative changes in the status of women over time in the area of rural development.

Yearbook of International Labour Statistics

Produced by the ILO, this includes gender-sensitive indicators on total and economically active population, employment and unemployment, hours of work, and wages. The ILO has also published a seven-volume series entitled *Sources and Methods:*

Labour Statistics, of which Volumes 2, 3, 4, 5 and 6 are of particular relevance.

World Bank

The World Bank publishes Social Indicators of Development on an annual basis. This publication provides sex-disaggregated indicators on: population, labour, education, enrolment ratios, life expectancy and maternal mortality. The main sources are the UN Statistical Office, ILO, and WHO, supplemented by national databases.

Other Donors

Developing Baseline Gender Indicators and Analysis for Country Program Planning: A Resource Guide. Hull: CIDA, Asia Branch, 1996

This Resource Guide includes:
+ a general discussion of the use of indicators at the country level;
+ indicator tables relating to political, economic, social and environmental gender-sensitive indicators at the country level;
+ factors which are likely to cause changes in indicators over time;
+ the availability of indicators by country, including data availability tables.

Notes

1   This draws on CIDA (1996a).

References

Adepoju, A and Oppong, C (eds.)(1994). *Gender, Work and Population in Sub-Saharan Africa*. London: James Currey.

Agarwal, B (1994). *A Field of One's Own: Gender and Land Rights in South Asia*. Cambridge: Cambridge University Press.

Alderman, H (1990). *Nutritional Status in Ghana and its Determinants*. Washington DC: World Bank, Social Dimensions of Adjustment in Sub-Saharan Africa, Working Paper No. 3.

Amnesty International (1995). *Human Rights Are Women's Rights*. New York: Amnesty International.

Anderson, V (1991). *Alternative Economic Indicators*. London: Routledge.

Anker, R (1994). "Measuring Women's Participation in the African Labour Force". In Adepoju, A and Oppong, C, 64-75.

Anker, R, Khan, M and Gupta, R (1988). *Women's Participation in the Labour Force: A Methods Test in India for Improving its Measurement*. Geneva: ILO, Women, Work and Development 16.

Boateng, E (1994). "Gender-Sensitive Statistics and the Planning Process". In Adepoju, A and Oppong, C, 88-111.

CEDAW (1991). "Consideration of Reports Submitted by States Parties under Article 18 of the Convention. Initial, Second and Third Periodic Reports of States Parties. Ghana". New York: UN, CEDAW/C/GHA/1-3.

CEDAW (1992). "Consideration of Reports Submitted by States Parties Under Article 18 of the Convention. Third Periodic Reports of States Parties. Canada". New York: UN, CEDAW/C/CAN/3.

CEDAW (1995a). "Progress Achieved in the Implementation of the Convention On The Elimination Of All Forms of Discrimination Against Women". New York: UN, Report by the Committee on the Elimination of Discrimination against Women, A/CONF. 177.7.

CEDAW (1995b). "Contributions of the Committee to International Conferences". New York: UN, Report by the Committee on the Elimination of Discrimination against Women, CEDAW/C/1995/7.

Census of India (1991). *Provisional Population Totals: Workers and Their Distribution*. Delhi: Registrar General of India, Paper 3 of 1991.

Chadeau, A (1993). "OECD Information Network on Non-Market Household Production". In Statistics Canada, 65-8.

CIDA (1996a). *Developing Baseline Gender Indicators and Analysis for Country Program Planning: A Resource Guide*. Hull: CIDA, Asia Branch (author Beck, T).

CIDA (1996b). *Guide to Gender-Sensitive Indicators*. Hull: CIDA, Policy Branch (authors Beck,T and Stelcner, M).

CIDA (1996c). *The Why and How of Gender-Sensitive Indicators: A Project Level Handbook*. Hull: CIDA, Policy Branch (authors Beck, T and Stelcner, M).

Commonwealth Secretariat and IWRAW (1996). *Assessing the Status of Women: A Guide to Reporting under the Convention on the Elimination of All Forms of Discrimination against Women*. London and Minnesota: Commonwealth Secretariat and IWRAW.

Commonwealth Secretariat (1999a). *Gender Mainstreaming in Education: A Reference Manual for Governments and Other Stakeholders*. Gender Management System Series. Authors: Leo-Rhynie, E and the Institute of Development and Labour Law, University of Cape Town. London.

Commonwealth Secretariat (1999b). *Using Gender-Sensitive Indicators: A Reference Manual for Governments and Other Stakeholders*. Gender Management System Series. London: Commonwealth Secretariat (author Beck,T).

Dey-Abbas, J and Gaiha, R (1993). "The Use of Socioeconomic Indicators for Evaluating Progress in Implementing the Programme of Action of the World Conference on Agrarian Reform and Rural Development". In Westendorff and Ghai, 234-60.

Dixon-Mueller, R (1987). *Women's Work in Third World Agriculture*. Geneva: ILO, Women, Work and Development 9.

Dreze, J and Sen, A (1989). *Hunger and Public Action*. Oxford: Oxford University Press.

Goetz, A and Sen Gupta, R (1996). "Who Takes the Credit? Gender, Power and Control over Loan Use in Rural Credit Programmes in Bangladesh". *World Development* 24 (1), 45-63.

Goldschmidt-Clermont, L (1987). *Economic Evaluations of Unpaid Household Work: Africa, Asia, Latin America and Oceania*. Geneva: ILO.

Harvey, A (1993). "Valuing the Unmeasured Economy: The Role of Time-Use Studies". In Statistics Canada, 77-85.

Inter-Secretariat Working Group (1993). *System of National Accounts*. Brussels: EC, OECD, IMF, UN and World Bank.

IWRAW (1988). *Assessing the Status of Women.* New York: International Women's Rights Action Watch.

Johnson, D (1985). "The Development of Social Statistics and Indicators on the Status of Women". *Social Indicators Research* 16, 233-61.

McGranahan, D et al (1985). *Measurements and Analysis of Socioeconomic Development: An Enquiry into International Indicators of Development and Quantitive Interrelations of Social and Economic Development.* Geneva: UNRSD.

Miller, C and Razavi, S (1997). "Conceptual Frameworks for Gender Analysis within the Development Context". Background paper, UNDP Gender Expert Group Meeting, New York, mimeo.

Moser, C (1993). *Gender Planning and Development: Theory, Practice and Training.* London: Routledge.

Murray, C (1993). "Development Data Constraints and the Human Development Index". In Westendorff and Ghai, 40-64.

Narayan, D and Nyamwaya, D (1996). *Learning from the Poor: A Participatory Assessment in Kenya.* Washington DC: World Bank Environment Department Paper No. 34.

Nelson, J (1996). *Feminism, Objectivity and Economics.* London: Routledge.

Statistics Canada (1978). *Estimating the Value of Household Work in Canada: 1971.* Ottawa: Statistics Canada (author Hawrylshyn, O).

Statistics Canada (1987). *Guide to Statistics Canada Data on Women.* Ottawa: Statistics Canada.

Statistics Canada (1992). *1996 Census Consultation Guide.* Ottawa: Statistics Canada.

Statistics Canada (1993). *International Conference on the Measurement and Valuation of Unpaid Work: Proceedings.* Ottawa: Statistics Canada, 89-532E.

Statistics Canada (1994). *1996 Census Consultation Report.* Ottawa: Statistics Canada.

Statistics Canada (1995a). *Census 1996: Questions and Reasons Why Questions Are Asked.* Ottawa: Statistics Canada.

Statistics Canada (1995b). *Households' Unpaid Work: Measurement and Valuation.* Ottawa: Statistics Canada, 13-603E, No. 3.

Statistics Canada (1995c). *Households' Unpaid Work: Measurement and Valuation.* Ottawa: Statistics Canada.

Status of Women Canada (1995). *Setting the Stage for the Next Century: The Federal Plan for Gender Equality.* Ottawa: Status of Women Canada.

UN (1984a). *Compiling Social Indicators on the Situation of Women.* New York: UN, Studies in Methods, Series F, No. 32.

UN (1984b). *Improving Concepts and Methods for Statistics and Indicators on the Situation of Women*. New York: UN, Studies in Methods, Series F, No. 33.

UN (1986). *Concepts and Methods for Integrating Social and Economic Statistics on Health, Education and Housing*. New York: UN, Studies in Methods, Series F, No. 40.

UN (1988a). *Improving Statistics and Indicators on Women Using Household Surveys*. New York: UN, Studies in Methods, Series F, No. 48.

UN (1988b). *Compendium of International Conventions Concerning the Status of Women*. New York: UN.

UN (1989). *Handbook on Social Indicators*. New York: UN, Studies in Methods, Series F, No. 49.

UN (1990a). *Handbook for National Statistical Data Bases on Women and Development*. New York: UN, Social Statistics and Indicators, Series K , No. 6.

UN (1990b). *Methods of Measuring Women's Participation and Production in the Informal Sector*. New York: UN, Studies in Methods, Series F, No. 46.

UN (1991). *The World's Women, 1970-1990: Trends and Statistics*. New York: UN, Social Statistics and Indicators, Series K, No. 8.

UN (1993). *Methods of Measuring Women's Economic Activity. Technical Report*. New York: UN, Studies in Methods, Series F, No. 59.

UN (1995a). *The World's Women 1995: Trends and Statistics*. New York: United Nations, Social Statistics and Indicators, Series K, No. 12.

UN (1995b). *World Summit for Social Development; Declaration and Programme for Action*. Copenhagen: UN.

UNDP (1995). *Human Development Report*. New York: Oxford University Press.

USAID (1994). *Country Gender Profiles: A Tool for Summarising Policy Implications from Sex-Disaggregated Data*. Washington DC: USAID.

Westendorff, D and Ghai, D (1993). *Monitoring Social Progress in the 1990s. Data Constraints, Concerns and Priorities*. Aldershot: Avebury.

World Bank (1994). *Enhancing Women's Participation in Economic Development*. Washington DC, World Bank Policy Paper.

World Bank (1995a). *Sectoral Indicators*. Washington DC: World Bank.

World Bank (1995b). *Towards Gender Equality*. Washington DC: World Bank.

.